Date: 11/16/11

J 613 .79 SAL
Salzmann, Mary Elizabeth,
Getting enough sleep /

Getting Enough Sleep

Mary Elizabeth Salzmann

Consulting Editor, Diane Craig, M.A./Reading Specialist

ABDO
Publishing Company

Published by ABDO Publishing Company, 4940 Viking Drive, Edina, Minnesota 55435.

Printed in the United States.

Credits
Edited by: Pam Price
Curriculum Coordinator: Nancy Tuminelly
Cover and Interior Design and Production: Mighty Media
Photo Credits: BananaStock Ltd., Image Source, ImageState, PhotoDisc, Stockbyte

Library of Congress Cataloging-in-Publication Data

Salzmann, Mary Elizabeth, 1968-
    Getting enough sleep / Mary Elizabeth Salzmann.
        p. cm. -- (Healthy habits)
    Includes index.
    Summary: Explains in simple language the importance of getting enough sleep.
    ISBN 1-59197-552-2
    1. Sleep--Juvenile literature. [1. Sleep.] I. Title.

RA786.S35 2004
613.7'9--dc22

2003057791

SandCastle™ books are created by a professional team of educators, reading specialists, and content developers around five essential components that include phonemic awareness, phonics, vocabulary, text comprehension, and fluency. All books are written, reviewed, and leveled for guided reading, early intervention reading, and Accelerated Reader® programs and designed for use in shared, guided, and independent reading and writing activities to support a balanced approach to literacy instruction.

Let Us Know

After reading the book, SandCastle would like you to tell us your stories about reading. What is your favorite page? Was there something hard that you needed help with? Share the ups and downs of learning to read. We want to hear from you! To get posted on the ABDO Publishing Company Web site, send us e-mail at:

sandcastle@abdopub.com

SandCastle Level: Transitional

Getting enough sleep
is a healthy habit.

Getting enough sleep means sleeping for at least ten hours.

Ten hours is a good night's sleep.

You feel good when you wake up after getting enough sleep.

It can be hard to pay attention in school if you don't get enough sleep.

You can feel too tired to play with your friends when you do not get enough sleep.

Beth reads a book at bedtime.

It helps her to fall asleep.

Kim sleeps better with her rabbit.

Tara likes her mom to read to her before she goes to sleep.

Evan listens to music at bedtime.

What do you do to get
a good night's sleep?

Did You Know?

It takes most people seven minutes
to fall asleep.

You burn more calories sleeping than
you do watching TV.

The largest hand-stitched teddy bear
ever made weighs 1,700 pounds and is
25 feet tall.

Giraffes only sleep for two hours a day.

King Louis XIV owned 413 beds.

Glossary

attention. the act of concentrating on or giving careful thought to something

bedtime. the time you usually go to sleep

habit. a behavior done so often that it becomes automatic

healthy. preserving the wellness of body, mind, or spirit

hour. 60 minutes

pay. to give or offer

school. a place where you go to be taught

About SandCastle™

A professional team of educators, reading specialists, and content developers created the SandCastle™ series to support young readers as they develop reading skills and strategies and increase their general knowledge. The SandCastle™ series has four levels that correspond to early literacy development in young children. The levels are provided to help teachers and parents select the appropriate books for young readers.

Emerging Readers
(no flags)

Beginning Readers
(1 flag)

Transitional Readers
(2 flags)

Fluent Readers
(3 flags)

These levels are meant only as a guide. All levels are subject to change.

To see a complete list of SandCastle™ books and other nonfiction titles from ABDO Publishing Company, visit www.abdopub.com or contact us at:

4940 Viking Drive, Edina, Minnesota 55435 • 1-800-800-1312 • fax: 1-952-831-1632